THE GOOD NEWS
ABOUT ARMAGEDDON

THE GOOD NEWS
ABOUT ARMAGEDDON

Steve McOrmond

Brick Books

Library and Archives Canada Cataloguing in Publication

McOrmond, Steve, 1971-
    The good news about Armageddon / Steve McOrmond.

Poems.
ISBN 978-1-894078-83-2

    I. Title.

PS8575.O74G66 2010   C811'.54   C2009-907387-0

Copyright © Steve McOrmond, 2010

We acknowledge the Canada Council for the Arts, the Government of Canada through the Book Publishing Industry Development Program (BPIDP), and the Ontario Arts Council for their support of our publishing program.

The cover image is a photograph called "Retro Television" taken by Shaun Lowe.

The author photograph was taken by Brad Marlin.

The book is set in Minion and Rotis.

Design and layout by Alan Siu.

Printed and bound by Sunville Printco Inc.

Brick Books
431 Boler Road, Box 20081
London, Ontario N6K 4G6

www.brickbooks.ca

For in the days before the flood, people were eating and drinking,
marrying and giving in marriage, up to the day Noah entered the ark;
and they knew nothing about what would happen
until the flood came and took them all away.

– Matthew 24:38-39

Come in. Be lost. Be still.
If you miss us at home
we'll be on our way to the reckoning.

– C.D. Wright

Contents

Advisory   9

The Good News about Armageddon   13

The Hypochondriac Flies to Mexico   51
When It Comes for You   52
Directions to the Ark   53
Night Figures   54
The Tunnel, the Light   55
Test Pattern   56
The End of the World   58
Autobiography   59

Strait Crossing   65

The Light Keepers   79
The Compensation of Art   80
Collision   81
The Secret Admirer   82
The Anorexic's Love Song   83
The Tooth Fairy's Lament   84

Penny Dreadful   86

The Poet   88

The Fortune Teller   90

I'd Like to Thank the Academy   92

Sleeper   94

Deuteronomy, Abridged   95

There Is a Chemical   97

Dark Clouds (Another Apocalypse)   98

Envoi   99

Notes and Acknowledgements   101

Biography   103

Advisory

1.0   The following program contains language and brief sexuality which some may find disturbing.

1.1   The following program may contain graphic content relevant to the development of character or to the advancement of the theme or plot.

1.2   Women's bare breasts; man's bare buttocks.

1.3   The following program may invite dangerous imitation, such as the use of plastic bags as playthings, or unsafe physical acts, such as climbing apartment balconies.

1.4   The following program may contain realistic scenes of violence which create the impression that violence is the preferred or only method to resolve conflict. The audience is advised to follow its programming.

1.5   People smoke. People snort drugs. Someone drowns.

1.6   The following program may contain domestic and civil disorders, scenes of destruction and accident. A coarse audience is intended.

1.7   The following program may deal casually with themes which could threaten the viewer's sense of security; e.g., the death or injury of parents, close relatives or pets.

1.8   Evidence of fatalism and irreligion; excessive special effects not required by the storyline.

1.9   The following program may contain scenes not suitable for language. The audience may contain violence not intended by the program.

2.0   People are assaulted; fighting; gunplay. Several car crashes; a fatal animal attack.

2.1   Objectionable words and phrases: Approx. 50.

The Good News about Armageddon

•

Young woman delivering the word
door to door: I was lonely, invited you in.

The time being short, we mustn't waste it,
drop of semen, speck of dust. Yada-yada.

My father's tanned arm out the car window, his hand
cupping the rush of cool air, then letting it go.

I have never met an angel, but I imagine
their wings under clothes, hymenopterous.

Here, my lucky number, sit a spell.
It will take awhile for the wave to reach us.

•

Up early, I'm at the computer,
the black cat on my lap, pressing the keys

with his toothy snout. These days
everyone has a novel in them.

We stayed out late last night,
me and my shadow. Our cups ranneth over.

Like Lazarus, I am risen. Grateful
and a little ashamed: what have I done

to deserve this day? The cat also
at a loss for words.

●

Old man, telling anyone who will listen
how you found Jesus, haven't

touched a drink in years, what makes you think
I'd want to be born again? Forgive me, Father,

I've watched too many wars, surfing between
car bombs and the canned laughter of a sitcom.

Who will man-up and take responsibility
for this moment, its casualties? *Anyone? Anyone?*

It's not the live footage but what's left,
the darkness outside the frame.

Let the record show the accused can't recall
the last time he did a good deed.   Duly noted.

•

As seen on TV, the president's limousine
moves only as fast as a man can walk.

My room is small, stale
with cigarettes. Yes, I've started again.

Death by cancer seems remote,
like worrying over a paper cut.

Behind the barricades, patriots
waving their stumps and hooks.

•

We come in from the city's rim: horse pasture
usurped by cul-de-sacs.

Walk left, stand right, please
use all available doors.

At this hour, we are
brain stems and meat.

North of here stood Finch's inn, The Bird in the Hand.
A travelling circus performed on the grounds.

Newspapers are ill at ease, falcons tethered to our fists.
Arabic, Cyrillic, Simplified Chinese.

We're all anonymous here.
Everyone has scuffed shoes.

•

Viagra, megaton, karoshi – how marvellous
the words my century has made.

My bad. I should learn to chill out
with a mochaccino, rightsize my rage.

Careful, the beverage you're about
to enjoy is extremely hot.

Love, I've given up on nearly everything –
black villages, 24-7, Taliban, TTYL.

Stay until the lights go out. Not if but when.

•

Why *this* Iraqi, *this* smart-bombed home?
A mind ill-equipped for multitudes.

River of fire pouring from a crack
in the sidewalk. Red ants swarming.

Any similarity to actual persons,
living or dead, is purely statistical.

Hippocrates said, "If you want
to be a surgeon, follow an army."

●

Morning: a cockroach halfway up the wall.
Evening and it hasn't budged an inch.

My thoughts need a bath,
my mouth a bar of soap.

How long since these hands
lent themselves?

I envy the one-legged man
reading the Qur'an on the subway.

He holds on and is moved.

•

The day has swollen ankles. We slow-mo
through thick, sulphurous air.

Done with healthy living, I'll have
the Creutzfeldt-Jakob with a side of fries.

We've smashed all the mirrors,
crossed and re-crossed the black cat's path.

Next, the ten commandments.
(I can never remember them all.)

If we summon the lightning,
maybe the rain will come too.

●

Forgive me my boredom as I forgive you
your pissiness. Angels should live alone.

Always at me with your chapter and verse.
La-la-la, I can't hear you. Come to bed.

I want to kiss the rosary of your spine,
take your prayer wheel out for a spin.

My muddy valentine, slip off
your thong of thongs. Anoint me.

•

Clever cricket, the harps on your wings
convince us you are many places at once.

Sitting on the dock, we raise our beers:
So long sirens, so long sky-view traffic report.

Can you hear that?
What?

The stars. They're pinging.
It hurts my ears.

●

Gonna get reacquainted with nature,
gonna take my Gore-Tex for a walk.

At dusk, the landscape loses definition,
tiny detonations in the brush.

Still a long piece from home, is this
Unknowing? A cloud of blackflies.

Let them come. Lift my sorry flesh
little by little into the sky.

•

On our last day, awakened
by the mechanized whine

we'd thought to leave behind.
The neighbours giving their lawn

a buzz cut. Riotous fecundity,
the air studded with spores.

•

What news from the provinces,
my toothless, one-eyed herald?

Tell me: are there signs of life
between the ruinous pillars of my legs?

Precious little, Milord. I counsel
you to conserve your strength:

downsize your harem, furlough
your wives and consorts.

Eminence, let your wisdom admit
nothing stirs you now, a tree with dead boughs.

Faithful servant, I know you speak
the truth, yet I long to be stirred.

Understand it's nothing personal.
Guards! Pummel his impertinent head.

•

Dem bones, dey be tellin'
tales, always de same ole.

De king wit de grievous wound
in his thigh, de trees wit no fruit.

Dem bones is all scratched up,
dey warble like wax cylinders.

It's a chore to listen, but listen
you must.

We grew fat, then very thin.
We drank from de chalice filled wit sand.

•

Online, I am no closer
to the blessed interconnectedness.

Deaf woman mauled by mountain lion.
Are Paris Hilton's 15 minutes over yet?

Outside, a cold wind scatters
the last of the fallen leaves.

Human disinterest story.
Corpse lay next to TV for 3 years.

This just in from Hubble: a pair of black holes
locked in death dance. Make it your screensaver.

Are we winning the war on terror?
I think it might snow.

•

9:30 in the morning and already
the cigarettes are whispering.

Leave me alone, I'm writing an ode
to the floating widget, trying to decipher

a coded communiqué: the lorem ipsum
of frost on the window pane.

The ones we love disappoint us,
and we them, so why even bother?

The chicken dances away, having mislaid
its head in the dust near the chopping block.

•

In the seedy washroom of the public house,
I stood wringing my hands.

G.H. Wood.
Sanitation for the Nation.

Wait a sec. Weren't we en route
to some kind of personal epiphany?

Bartender, don't
be a stranger: hit me again.

And now a word
from our sponsor... *Kills bugs dead.*

We are an argument
for unintelligent design.

Even the cartoon cockroach
up there on the plasma must pity us:

How soft and fragile,
their bones on the inside.

•

Nigh, nigh. The storefronts
proclaim it: *Final Days! 50-70% Off.*

In the YouTube video, two women
vomit into each other's mouths.

Among other things, real or simulated.
You're skinning the cat, I'm just holding its tail.

On a beach in Western Australia, 90 whales
crushed by the weight of their own bodies.

How like you to turn your low spirits
into a global crisis. Must everything reflect?

Jesus Saves, intones the guy with the goitre.
Mon amie, Monsanto, my soul is Roundup Ready.

All I ever wanted was God, a hereafter
and 72 virgins. Yes, that'll do.

•

She wants to talk about having a baby.
I peer under umbrellas for my ex's red hair.

She has nursed sick and wounded animals
back to health. I have torn the wings off flies.

She is at the centre of a vast social network.
I've gone days without speaking.

She likes to be the last to leave a party.
I want to get home before the end of time.

She lies down in fresh snow to make an angel.
I unzip my fly and write my name.

●

If a house, a teardown.
If a car, a moving violation.

AS IS soaped on the windshield,
you know I'm no bargain.

Leave and I'll have to learn
to go out and meet women.

So what if I fell for the Good Book
in your hand, the nicotine patch

on your bare arm? Never could
tell the blood from the wine.

•

Today, another march on the capital.
I lie in bed with the remote, thinking of Rome

before the fall. Such are the luxuries
afforded the conscientious bystander.

Egyptian cotton sheets with a high thread count.
What more can one ask in a time of war?

Full of arthritis, the black cat
curls its spine and sleeps.

•

In the heat-shimmering arroyos, small oases
of plant life where Mexicans have died of thirst.

The esteemed poet nods coolly, picks his teeth.
We are better people on the page.

He walks into the sun, shedding his clothes.
The manufacturer has issued a recall.

These bones are of a mind it's quitting
time.   Someone,

light a match under this little pile of sticks.

•

I went out, the street lights haloed,
impossible whiteness of new snow.

Vincible me, 3 weeks
without a drop of courage.

At last, the clouded surface
begins to clear.

It was then the apparition
appeared to me, a blur

like hummingbird wings,
a doorway in the falling snow.

Come, child, it said, if you would
be healed. Walk to me.

•

The roll call of extinctions is televised.
What are you waiting for? Stand.

Our Lady of the Imminent
Catastrophe, I beg you: not yet.

One of these days, we're going to get
our shit together. We're going to

rise. I've seen it written in a fortune cookie:
The axe doesn't fall far from the tree.

When there are no more wolves,
what will you cry then?

Today's the feast day of St. John of God,
patron saint of hospitals and alcoholics.

I think that calls for a drink, don't you?
Let's celebrate with meat and mirth,

wine and tankards of ale, for tomorrow
we might not be able to get out of bed.

If dancing's your thing, then do it now.
Yogi Berra: "It gets late early out there."

I know a woman who claims each night
her dead husband comes to kiss her eyes.

We are as wisps of hair caught in brambles,
our presence loaned to us by the wind.

∙

Keeping pace with the Freightliner
up ahead, shadowing its tail lights.

11 hours I've been driving.
When will I learn to bring enough CDs?

O Captain of the Trans-Canada, tonnage drifting
over the line, will we make Fredericton tonight?

You might be carrying frozen turkeys, microchips,
tractor steering assemblies, creamed corn.

I'm tired, good buddy,
and fain would pull o'er to snooze.

Do women really expose their breasts?
I'll bet they do, though seldom, too seldom.

•

Pre-op: chest shaved, star-crossed,
a tree marked for the chainsaw.

Father, don't you understand? I'm not ready.
Try thinking about somebody else for a change.

In the space of a cigarette, we may be spared
or else a trumpet brings down the house.

One minute you're watching the Doppler
on The Weather Channel, next the roof's gone.

You're rooting among splintered joists, torn sheets
of drywall for the good silverware, the dog.

Near the hospital's back door, a pair of crows,
two black lungs discarded in the snow.

•

Out past the chevrons, the car radio
has only one thing on its mind.

Potsherd, flint arrowhead, green circuit board.
A funny thing happened on the way to the landfill.

Don't worry about the compass,
I wouldn't know how to read it anyway.

The sky's misbehaving, hailstones pocking
the hood, little stars in the windshield.

Leave a trail of crumbs. I'll be along soon.
A half hour later in Newfoundland.

•

More signs: the germs in my kitchen.
This morning, a dead crow.

C'est la vie, c'est le fin de la vie.
And some were rising; others just

falling to sleep. In these hours of prolific
doubt, how will we acquit ourselves?

The narcissist googles himself *ad infinitum*.
The torturer whistles while she works.

Shall I tend the garden,
or let it grow up in weeds?

If you can't save the world,
then perhaps you should leave.

•

To the rich uncle who told me to get a life,
this change purse, a repurposed bull scrotum.

To certain past employers
(you know who you are)

whom I wouldn't give
the sweat off my balls,

I bequeath
the sweat off my balls.

To the abstinent, a glass of moonshine;
to the earnest, my fart machine.

The cabin I leave to the elements, lake
to the herons, the sweep net of their attention.

To you, my long-suffering
lover, a crow feather, its rainbow sheen.

And to our friends, nothing but words words words,
the worn-out stub of my name.

•

Despite the catastrophists'
almanac, another spring.

It comes in time-lapse,
an avalanche in reverse.

The hills green up, the valleys
spread their long legs, alluvial

fields wet and raw.
I'm so horny I could cry.

A morning wrapped in cellophane
like a fresh pack of smokes.

In the spruce, a white-throated
sparrow tunes up, one phrase

over and over, history
repeating itself.

•

Desire goes to the dentist,
can't sleep for the ache in its jaw.

Was she flesh or god filament, I'll never
know. Tomato, toe-maw-toe.

My mission bell, my mercy fuck,
my watchtower, my Kyoto.

We met at a courtly love convention.
She undid her hair and I fell.

•

Went out to buy cigarettes, came home
with a 5-lb mesh bag of oranges.

How does one survive? Improvise,
improvise. Today I will get out of bed, wash, eat.

Whether this presumes
a future I can't say.

In the desert of the kitchen table,
the oranges, a burning bush.

O Spring!
A woman holding her skirt down in the wind.

•

What keeps me here?
Only the simplest things.

Getting up to take a leak,
I meet the old cat in the hall.

He yawns, I yawn, running
my fingers up and down his back.

A short circuit, the darkness
crackling with sparks.

The Hypochondriac Flies to Mexico

The plane is sick. Feverish chills
shudder through its aluminum skin.
The hatch hums closed, a stopper
in a test tube of plague. En route to takeoff,
the pilot's nasal drawl, "Thank you for flying
Pandemic Air." The plane is sick. It hobbles aloft,
the landing gear withdraws into the belly
like shocked testicles. Seated on the aisle, I squint
down the length of the cabin: human convection plumes,
germ haloes. The woman in the window seat
makes three trips to the restroom in an hour – Adenovirus,
Norwalk, dysentery? The plane is sick,
its cargo contagion. My throat
abraded by recycled air, the stuporous quiet
by a child's sobs and tubercular wheezes,
I want to say, with the time that is left,
I always loved you, would have followed
you anywhere. Squeeze my hand.
See how our words
trail into coughs?

When It Comes for You

Implacable as a building superintendent,
patient as smallpox, it won't

care about your works in progress,
patents pending, or how you spent

your summer vacation. Never mind
the unpaid parking tickets in the glovebox,

your fondness for malt liquor.
The bland face of an insurance adjuster,

canned responses from a telemarketer's script.
It's heard everything before, absorbing your pleas

like a bouncer at a nightclub. *But I never learned
to tie a sheepshank or how a bill becomes a law...*

The vacant gaze of a drive-thru attendant,
the deaf ears of rain. You've had all the time

in the world to master the semicolon,
teach the dog to shake a paw, or

just once, to use the word *pellucid*
to describe your beloved's eyes, but no,

that isn't the right one either.

Directions to the Ark

First right after the abattoir.

Night Figures

Crescent moon,
a shut-in's toenail.

                                      Silence, pouring out
                                      its life story.

Cold, bone's
tuning fork.

                                      Whisky, olfactory
                                      chiaroscuro.

Darkness, a gloved hand
pressed over the mouth.

                                      Telephone, at this hour
                                      must be bad news.

The Tunnel, the Light

Poorly provisioned for this world,
I wanted to believe in another.

When I came close to dying, God
was nowhere near.

To have heard the voice within
the void commanding: Go back

to your wilderness of ordinary things.
Then how sure my steps.

Sometimes, when they sew you up,
they leave behind a clamp, bit of sponge

or a careless intern's hoop earring.
The flesh has its way, a tree

growing around and through
the mesh of a chain-link fence.

Sometimes an organ is removed
in error. Healthy kidney

instead of the diseased one, good eye
mistaken for its milky counterpart.

Perhaps that explains my slow recovery.
Neither here nor there.

There were hands inside my chest.
They replaced my heart with a bag of stones.

Test Pattern

Hunkered down on the couch, brain
refusing to follow the body into sleep,

or vice versa. The no man's land
between 3 and 4 in the morning.

Heat lightning over the lake,
Turner meets Van de Graaff.

Thumb on the flicker, I receive
the world on a wide band of channels.

Paid announcements for countertop rotisseries,
knives that slice through beer cans like butter,

diet pills, Bowflex. Right now, beautiful
young women are waiting to take my call.

I had hoped to stumble across
some sci-fi flick from the cold war,

We come in peace, but it's much too late,
most stations have suspended

their programming, NTSC colour bars,
the continuous 1,000 Hz monotone,

which is the frequency of the dead,
informationless.

At a certain age, 7 or 8,
my vision was better than 20/20.

I could see the monster in the closet,
the yellow slits of its eyes.

Everything feels in focus,
though the lenses are a little dusty,

blind spots, scotomata. Now the monsters
are out of the closet and the wolves

wear wolves' clothing. The sky flares,
bright as phosphorus, over

before it began.

The End of the World

The persistent cough, the routine procedure,
the congenital defect, the faulty wiring,
the fire in the starboard engine, the *force majeure*,
the mistress in the city, the last spirited thrust,
the little breeze off the coast of Africa,
the apples torn from the trees,
the unopened mail, the paper boy ringing the bell,
the atmospheric anomaly, the snow on the TV,
the hot wind with its tincture of rotting fish,
the wasp's nest of tumours, the drug-resistant strain,
the feeding tube, the shunt, the morphine drip,
the fatigue and general malaise,
the night inventory of the medicine cabinet,
the sleeping pills, the razor blades,
the reversals suffered as a child,
the bend in the road, the patch of black ice,
the telephone pole advancing in the high beams,
the statistical improbability, the cougar attack,
the stray piece of cosmic debris, the locals celebrating
the wedding of the loveliest girl in the village
by firing their guns into the air.

Autobiography

The night the old movie house burned
to the ground was the coldest of the year,

water from the firemen's hoses
flash-froze before it reached the flames,

otherworldly arcs of ice. A lousy place to start,
but I can go back later and revise.

The washed-out quality of those days, faded
wood panelling, hum of fluorescent tubes.

Leftovers on the stove, dirty dishwater
in the sink; my folks arguing again.

One minute I'm playing the pots and pans,
the next, I'm laid out on the linoleum, his arm

caught in mid-air, petrified. Stop, rewind,
playback. Is that a tear in the statue's eye?

No, I don't want fire and ice, my father's
90 proof breath. More than that

is hard to say. The story should begin
before I was born: It's Saturday night

at the officers' mess, fly boys banking sharply
on the dance floor, blue mist of saxophones.

A big band plays Cab Calloway
like there's no tomorrow, the musicians

sweating through their shirts, and my parents,
he in uniform, she a pale green dress,

sway in each other's arms, her cheek
against his shoulder, his hands clasped

at the small of her back, awkward and careful
as though cupping a newborn's head.

Warning.
Injury and death have rewarded
careless sightseers here.

– Plaque, Peggy's Cove Lighthouse

Strait Crossing

•

Waiting to board the ferry, we watch an ill wind
pounce on a black truck tarpaulin,
sink its teeth in and pull.
                              If we heeded
such vague forebodings, we'd never
get anywhere.
Soon the traffic attendants
will zip past on their scooters, fluorescent
orange vests, those batons
used to guide jets
safely to their gates.
                        Empty,
the *MV John Hamilton Gray*
sits high in the water, straining
against ropes thicker than a man's forearm.
We'll supply the ballast.

•

We've barely left, the jetty
sliding past us like a film strip,
foghorn clearing its throat,
when a sound like a shovel
dragged over gravel
shudders through the decks;
equipment shifts in cabinets, cutlery
skitters across tables, clattering
onto the floor.   A caught breath,
then nervous laughter: We're ok,
aren't we? The captain on the PA:
An unexpected gust…
we should be underway
momentarily.

•

Weighing in
at 10,000 tonnes, propelled by
8 Fairbanks Morse 12-cylinder
engines, the *Gray*'s hardened hull
makes ice shatter like an ageing welterweight's
glass jaw, grinds
it into jagged slabs,
                            black water
boiling up through the cracks.
But not today.
                Stuck fast
on a shoal between the breakwater
and the Borden docks, 16,000 horses
can't drag us off the sand.

•

     Before it's finished,
this gale will sheer metal
siding from the boatsheds, push
miles inland, flip 2 tractor-trailers
onto their sides.
     It will do to us
         anything it chooses.

•

5 hours,
        still stranded,
the harbour lights just
out of reach. 116 passengers, 31 crew.
Last-minute Christmas shoppers
bound for Moncton, a retired couple
driving south to spend the winter,
and a young woman travelling alone
to the hospital in Halifax.
If she doesn't make it,
her mother will have to die
without her.

•

Ferrying
between past and present:
your first trip to the Island,
February, and very cold.
On the boat, we stayed outside, shivering
the whole 9 miles across.
The *Gray*'s engines pounding, more felt
than heard, and the deeper groan of ice
riding up against the bow,
                        hairline
                                fractures
                zig-
zagging across the white sheet. How
one winter the ice
came ashore at Hampton,
                        nudged
the Greens' cottage off its foundation, depositing it
half a mile down the beach
without so much as knocking
the salt and pepper shakers off the shelf.
                                      Sipping
your double-double, you looked
quietly thrilled as though reading
of this in a book.

•

Numb, my mind
slips its moorings.
                    The Age of Sail,
fish so thick you could
walk on water, never
get your feet wet.
                      A pretty story.
No one knows how many
vessels were lost. No lighthouses
anywhere on the Island, the colony
balking at the expense. No fishery of its own
to speak of, and no desire to serve
the American fleet. When a storm blew up,
the men from Gloucester had nowhere to go.
10 or 12 ships anchored together,
the winds driving one against the other,
                                  a Sargasso
of masts and riggings.

•

River Bell, Golden Grove, May Queen, Gypsy,
their names rise out of the sea.
                                      The *Arrival*
eastward of Cape Kildare, *Fair Play*
in Tracadie Harbour, *Kohinoor*
at Hillsborough Bay.
                            H.M. Alert,
The Golden Rule, Agenora, Flirt,
Star of the Sea, Star of the East, Polar Star,
the barque *Nantucket*, the 35-tonne *Realty*.
Mary Lenore, Clara Jane, Jenny Lind, Helen Mar.
The schooner *Mary F. Pyke*, her burnt
ribs jutting from the sand below
Beaton's Point.
                          Charlos Augusta,
Marmion, Cymbria, Urdine, Foam,
Mantamora, Genesta, Naiad, Nettle,
Pow Hatten, Vulture, Yarrow,
Orpheus, Olga, Sovinto,
Dominion.

•

                  Let us heave to,
play gin rummy, tell
dirty jokes and stories we know
by heart, share a laugh
                        at the expense
of progress, how our technology fails us
spectacularly. Let us pray.

•

If the wind lessens, they'll risk
taking us off in inflatable boats.
The long-haul truckers, smitten
with the notion of going down
with the ship, vow
to stay with their vehicles.
                                        You admire
the *esprit de corps*, the chrome-plated
balls. These men
pitting their jocular banter
against the deadpan profundity of the sea.
                                        But you wonder
how long it would last out on deck, first
the brave words, then their owners
swept over the side.

●

It will be three days
before the last passenger
comes safely ashore.
The video lottery machines
go on playing their tinny music;
though their bellies are full,
                         the men
keep feeding them.

•

                A boy stands alone
at the window,
                      water and sky,
no demarcation. His breath
fogs the glass and he wipes it
with his small fist. He has the look of one
who understands how suddenly
the bottom drops. He knows what the lungs know:
                          The day
you think you can swim forever
is the day you drown.

The Light Keepers

After the storms abated and the sun shone,
we realized we were not alone.

Others had survived, in train tunnels,
sub-basements and sewers.

Once we found we could breathe the air,
there was work to be done: food, water, wood.

Stockbrokers, bike couriers, cooks and clerks
rediscovered the art of the longbow.

We had shelters and cisterns to build, gardens
to plant and tend, canned goods to forage.

The city, our little fires, visible for miles.
Though much was poisoned, much persists.

Somehow the young lovers find one another,
crunch of broken glass underfoot

as they lean into each other in the sooty dark.
Everything before now, a rehearsal.

Shyly, she traces the worry lines etched
on his face; he the scars on her wrists.

From less than this, civilizations have risen:
a man, a woman, a wing, a prayer.

Every few days now, another Moses comes,
leading his or her people across the cinder plain.

The Compensation of Art

A man with a patch over his eye
upon which is painted an eye.

Collision

The man, staked out
on the steps of the Starbucks,
clapping his hands, stamping his feet
to ward off the cold, is not
my disembodied conscience,
nor a woodblock by Dürer.
He is not the human condition.
It's snowing. Huge wet flakes
stick to the man's coat,
muffle the traffic sounds.
All those cars streaming
almost silently into the core.
I'm not fully awake yet,
haven't sipped from the cup
that urges me to *be exceptional*.
Fumbling in my pocket for change,
I hand it over gingerly, bracing
for impact; how my gaze
skids across his face, his across mine,
fishtailing to avoid the eyes.

The Secret Admirer

I know your moods, the scent on your wrist.
I know when you have cares, you care to walk,
often by the sea. You would not recognize me.
I am neither short nor tall, handsome nor ugly;
when I enter a room, it is even more empty.
Born on the night of a tire fire, my life doesn't
smell like roses. Calamity and I have a way
of coinciding. You needn't worry. I'm content
to linger in parking garages and coffee shops;
eyes that follow in crowds at the mall, fingers
that barely graze your hair. At close range,
words congeal in my throat. One fine day,
I'll find the courage, the perfect moment.
Until then, I'll run silent, at a safe distance,
attached to you by a thin, invisible wire.

The Anorexic's Love Song

You can touch me, I promise
I won't break.

Haven't you ever lit a fire
with flint and steel?

When the flesh evaporates, the bones
that are left grow harder.

Think of a gourd, hollowed out,
the skin like lacquered armour.

Grasp the polished knobs
of my shoulders, push

my hips ajar. I am all blunt edges.
Come, bruise yourself.

If I cry out, it's only because
I'm floating away, filled with helium.

If you wish to find me,
check the ceiling.

The Tooth Fairy's Lament

None of the cachet of the fat man
in the red suit. I am soon forgotten,
obsolete. Nobody rides around in

carriages anymore, much less one
studded with milk teeth, enamel
gleaming coldly in the moonlight.

It isn't easy working nights;
one is always tired, slave
to circadian rhythms.

No colleagues, no banter
around the water cooler
to keep one sane. I fear

I've become a strange old bird,
stealing into a child's room
after dark, lifting her little head

off the pillow, fumbling beneath.
Should she wake, a flick of my wand
and she'll be wood again…

Forgive me, girl, I didn't mean
to frighten you. I'm not good
with children. May I

offer a crumb of advice
before I put you under?
This won't be the last of life's

exfoliations. We go on exchanging
bits of ourselves, and for what?
A few coins, something sweet.

It's right your tongue should worry
itself raw. Though a new incisor
already cuts the gum, this is still a loss.

Youth is what we all covet; be careful
how you dispose of yours.
Many would use it against you, cast spells.

A tooth may be buried, swallowed
or salted and burned; I prefer them
strung around my neck like pearls.

Penny Dreadful

You can tell it's a fellah writing,
they never get the clothes right.

On the cover, I'm gussied up in hoop skirt
and crinoline. I never had no Sunday best.

I dressed like a man, rode like one too.
And I stunk of horse near as bad.

Run off with the rancher's son, it's true,
but that ain't the half of it. The boy

was prettier than me, loose wrists,
if you know what I mean. His mamma

in heaven and alls the old man could do was
kick the snot out of him any chance he got.

When the bastard said he'd sooner die
than watch his son consort with trash,

I was happy to oblige, hit him 'cross the neck
with the cast-iron fry pan, still greasy

from bacon and grits. Now you get
a wagonload of clichés: sagebrush,

chaparral, spine-tipped leaves
of the Joshua tree. The book writer

laying it on thick and poetical. The boy and me
lighting out through the cinematic tumbleweeds.

Ain't it ripe? Still, there's a flyspeck of truth
in that shitstorm of lies. The boy was innocent.

When the knife ran away with the spoon, I was
the knife. We robbed filling stations, mom-and-pops,

worked up to banks. If anyone got in the way,
they got pistol-whipped. Or worse.

The boy made a piss-poor accomplice. No great hell
as a lover neither. He done what he was told.

I was a dog who'd got a taste for chickens.
I'd keep at it till someone put me down.

We moved around, sun tearing at our eyes,
desert floor the colour of tanned hide.

The voices in my head wouldn't quit:
Stick the pen-knife in his back. Ride.

The Poet

The poet, who I have it on authority
enjoys tequila reposado and group sex,

ought to write more interesting poems.
Too many trees, and he no swinger of birches.

To read his poetry is to grasp that the wisdom
of the ages is lost on us, misfiled somewhere

in the office of obscure patents. To describe
the way the light falls on this surface or that

is not the same thing as enlightenment.
What to do now with my signed copy, purchased

from the author in a moment of weakness?
Pass it along to an acquaintance, he'll doubt

my discernment, if not our friendship.
Banish the book to the purgatory of a low shelf,

it will infect the air with mediocrity. Already
I have a low-grade fever, sense that a band of

colour – yellow, perhaps? – has vanished
from the spectrum. Soon all will be grey-scale.

Set the words to music, perfect for piping
into elevators, waiting rooms, the tune

that comes over the line when someone
you hope to impress puts you on hold.

Burn it in the firepit, the pages smoke like green wood,
and the gods, who invented orgies, wrinkle their noses,

the stale odour of inconsequence. Throw it in the lake,
fish go belly up and little turtles, en masse,

leave their lily pads and begin the long, slow trek
overland to more hospitable waters.

The Fortune Teller

1

In Mexico City on the Street of Diviners,
I had the ear of generals and narco-lords.
Here, it's mostly giggly girls and soccer moms
out for a lark. Up the creaky steps they come
in twos or little packs. Go ahead and laugh,
soon we'll be knee-deep in your fears.
Please, sit. I'll just be a moment.
I fuss with cups and saucers like a geisha,
all the time listening. The loose Darjeeling
warms them up. People have no idea what a word
or gesture can convey. Their cups empty,
the cards shuffled and arranged: Now,
let's pull back the curtain, shall we?

2

Just because I'm getting paid doesn't mean
I'll let them make a mockery of my mother's gift.
This one keeps interrupting, either too drunk
or too vapid to hold her tongue.
I grab her wrist so hard it'll leave a mark.
In the mountains where I was born,
a type of hummingbird appears
each fall to pass the winter. Scarcely heavier
than bees, they travel from Alaska, pulled
across the skies by something we cannot see.
We too are guided by invisible forces, the lover
to her beloved, the murderer to his murderee.
Trajectories. Objects in motion. Chances are.
I wonder if you've thought this through?
You might not like what you hear.

3.

It's the cold I can't abide. Even in summer,
my feet are blocks of ice. Turn up the electric
heater, watch it glow. Where were we?
Oh, yes, the boyfriend…Will he…Should you…
I close my eyes, reach into the black,
pluck a jewel. This one looks harmless enough.

4.

A man's footsteps in the stairwell, slow and heavy.
The desperate ones show up late and alone.
I brace myself for the weight of withholding.
Nobody wants a bad fortune. Shy, awkward,
he leans against the door jamb, out of breath
from the climb. He is young, tall and very, very thin.
It doesn't take any special powers to know
what his red bandanna is meant to conceal.
Not everyone grows old. I'm sorry, dear,
I was just about to close. Tonight, the cards
are unhappy, the tea leaves aren't talking,
at least not to me. He pivots, shakily,
like a man on stilts and without a word
descends the noisy steps to the street.
Sometimes, despite myself, I do see.

I'd Like to Thank the Academy

One last thing before they cue
the music and cut to commercial…

Actors are always talking about method.
I never had one. A few moments

watching an old man with a limp
and I had it memorized, just knew

the daily indignities: dragging his obstinate limb
up the bus steps, sighing when a young

woman offers her seat: You are too kind.
I was an empty vessel, waiting to be filled up

with second-hand feelings. Screenwriters
put foolish words in my mouth and you

folks at home believed them. Bums in seats.
I should have run for president.

No, acting was the easy part. It was the rooms
full of tinselly talk, perfect teeth. Like climbing K2,

one needs time to adjust to that rarefied air.
Startled by the bidet in Paris, tumbling

out of a stretch limo in NYC. I won't bore you
with the details – O the stucco and vinyl-sided

misery of that little town where I got my start –
but suffice to say, nothing had prepared me.

Tasting a glass of wine in a fancy restaurant
while the waiter hovers over my shoulder, fizzy

animation but with underpinnings of street life.
Simply exquisite, *garçon*, now fuck off.

Pardon my French. You've seen the tabloids
in line at the checkout: excess was always my MO.

Hard to pass up a line of coke when it lies
on a starlet's airbrushed ass like a landing strip.

I'd circle for awhile, then point my nose down.
White pills to fall asleep, little blue ones to get it up.

Priapism an occupational hazard – for that,
the good doctor can make a house call.

Never mind my recent work goes straight
to video and the housewives from Kansas

no longer write me love letters. I can't complain.
I've got this glorified slo-pitch trophy and a new liver.

The old one, preserved in formaldehyde,
should fetch a pretty penny on eBay.

If I wasn't Botoxed, I'd be grinning ear to ear.

Sleeper

Between stations, the tunnel loops,
pig-scream of inertia, the driver riding the brake.
It's 7 in the morning, winter darkness above
and beneath. The woman slumps in her seat,
her body swaying with the lurch and lean.
How far she has propelled herself beyond
simple exhaustion, and with such a burden:
shoulders, eyes, corners of the mouth;
everything droops. Not enough time
to put herself together, hair still damp
from the shower, gessoed with mousse.
Her coat is open. In her haste, she's left
the top button of her blouse undone; the rise and fall
of her chest, that bone chapel, an intimacy
she'd likely never intend. Overhead
the blown speaker squawks, the doors open and close,
cold subterranean gusts, much shuffling of feet, still
she does not wake. At the end of the line,
if she doesn't come to, someone will lay a hand
lightly on her arm. You must admit, this mercy
is a little strained. Were she to miss her stop,
the train reversing, carrying her back home,
what'd be the harm? Would the mighty engine
of commerce shudder and seize, the shipment
remain stuck in customs, the territory manager
make his own coffee or do without?
Spare her the kinship. Let her sleep.

Deuteronomy, Abridged
(after Robert Bringhurst)

We skirted their encampments by night,
the soldiers drunk, preoccupied

with rape or dreams of rape.
And the tide favoured us. Small wonder.

Nothing had prepared us for the desert.
We walked. The weak sickened and died.

I went up the mountain to escape
the heat, to clear my head and think.

Aaron in charge, cooking up his own schemes.
We are a pliable people, drawn

like magpies to glittery things. Whatever works
to keep them moving: carrot, switch,

carrot. One thing I know: the meek are never
blessed; they ask for little, receive less.

Altitude sickness, but no visions.
When I finally decided to come down,

what message could I bring? The women
and children careworn and hungry, the truth

hard to swallow. They needed hope,
my lies the next best thing.

Out of danger, their bellies full of bread and wine,
they can make up their own minds.

The burning bush was just a bush.
The stones, stones.

I climbed above the clouds
and found nothing there.

There Is a Chemical

There is a chemical that induces acute
euphoria. Just 20 parts per million
in a municipal water supply, and no one shows up
for work at the Velcro factory. Security guards
desert their posts, the Wal-Mart greeter
pushes a long train of shopping carts
down the parkway, signalling with his hands
to change lanes. Hyperactivity, recklessness
in the operation of a motor vehicle
or dangerous machinery. One's mind
races in endless tangents, speech tumbles over
itself, fragmented, broken. The faces of those
affected are said to be dumbstruck,
orgasmic. Side effects include dry mouth,
difficulty sleeping, increased sex drive, rashes
or hives. Although the results of exposure
are well-documented, the specific regions
of the mammalian brain that mediate them
remain largely unknown. Injected into the *nucleus
accumbens* of Sprague Dawley rats, the drug
inhibits swimming and escape behaviour.
Colourless, odourless, it was developed
to suppress insurgency, soften targets.
Less than a thimbleful and we'd happily
greet our liberation, grinning
as the bombs shower down
and the ground troops advance.

Dark Clouds (Another Apocalypse)

The clouds rolled in and never left.
Lightning in them but no rain.

Life, as Auden observed, went on
disinterestedly. There was the tuna

casserole to keep from burning, the dog
whimpering to be let out.

Panels of experts convened on TV
to discuss the subterranean rumblings,

the preponderance of messianic cults.
We perked up at the gory bits,

the jumpers and self-immolations,
rituals involving goat's blood.

Accustomed to instant gratification,
we wanted our apocalypse now.

How many times could we say goodbye
before we grew bored, turned a blind eye?

We had fetishes to attend to,
money to make and spend.

Years since we'd seen the stars,
they ceased to cross our minds.

No, never
any rain.

Envoi

What advice can I give, my fledglings,
my little vanishings, as you pack your things
and prepare to leave? Everything is fine, the sky
has been falling a long time. My wisdom in short
supply, these words must seem vague and kitschy
like the Lord's Prayer painted on a grain of rice.
Already you are better than me. Each generation
is and should be incomprehensible to its parents.
We will want to go quietly. Don't let our grey hair
keep you from meting out the judgment we're due.
Love immoderately and permit yourselves rage.
Anger makes things happen. The mob is gospel.
And to those who claim it couldn't be stopped:
At every point along its path, the arrow is still.

Notes and Acknowledgements

Some of these poems first appeared, often in earlier incarnations, in *The Antigonish Review*, *Arc*, *Bei Mei Feng* (China), *CV2*, *Event*, *fhole*, *The Moosehead Anthology 10: Future Welcome* (Montreal: DC Books, 2005), *Grain*, *I.V. Lounge Nights* (Toronto: Tightrope, 2008), *Jacket* (Australia), *The New Quarterly*, *Nuit Blanche: Poems for Late Nights* (Toronto: RSS Press, 2007), *The Peter F. Yacht Club*, *poetrypei.com*, *poetry'z own*, *Prairie Fire*, *PRISM international* and *Riddle Fence*. My thanks to the editors of these publications.

Thanks to all who, in various ways, helped to shape these poems: Julie and Ian Dennison, Adam Dickinson, Adrienne Barrett Hofman, Robert and Margaret Hoops, Ken Howe, Jessica Johnson, Anita Lahey, Richard Lemm, Steve Noyes, John Reibetanz, David Seymour, Charmaine and Matthew Tierney, Andy Weaver and Jan Zwicky.

Thanks and enduring love, as always, to Janet who, for some reason, didn't want a book about the end of the world dedicated to her.

I am eternally grateful to John Smith for the hours spent on the telephone discussing poetry and much else.

Special thanks to my editor Don McKay and to everyone at Brick Books.

My thanks to Shaun Lowe for the cover photograph and to Adriana Afford of Argyle Fine Art (http://www.argylefa.tk).

The Canada Council for the Arts, the Ontario Arts Council and the Toronto Arts Council provided financial support during the completion of this book.

The poem "When It Comes for You" received a "Highly Commended" award in the 2005 Petra Kenney International Poetry Competition.

"Advisory" takes liberties with two base texts: *The Voluntary Code Regarding Violence in Television Programming* developed by the Canadian Association of Broadcasters and the parental guidance found on a rental DVD copy of *Adaptation*, Dir: Spike Jonze, 2002.

"Envoi" is the traditional address of the poet to his or her poem or book of poems before sending it out into the world.

The book's second epigraph is by C.D. Wright, from "The Secret Life of Musical Instruments," *Steal Away: Selected and New Poems* (Port Townsend, WA: Copper Canyon Press, 2002).

"Strait Crossing" is for Geoffrey Green.

"The Hypochondriac Flies to Mexico" is for Janet McOrmond.

Steve McOrmond is the author of two previous books of poetry. His first collection, *Lean Days* (2004), was shortlisted for the Gerald Lampert Award. His second book, *Primer on the Hereafter* (2006), was awarded the Atlantic Poetry Prize. His work also appears in the anthology *Breathing Fire 2: Canada's New Poets*. Originally from Prince Edward Island, he now lives in Toronto.